# AVIATION PIONEER

## FIRST FLIGHT TO INDIA 1919

GORDON STEWART

# AVIATION PIONEER

## THE FIRST UK FLIGHT TO INDIA AND ASSISTANCE IN ENDING THE THIRD AFGHAN WAR

A celebration of the life of Sergeant Thomas Brown 313642 and fellow RAF flight heroes who navigated the first through-flight 1919 journey. It also highlights his involvement in the third Afghan war.

*Sergeant Thomas Brown*

*Handley Page V/1500*

# INTRODUCTION

Sergeant Thomas Brown was a humble man and rarely spoke of the exploits you are about to read in this book. Diaries, documents and artefacts were discovered that gave insight into Brown's and the flight crew's achievements. The context of Britain today in the 21st Century is very different to the British Empire of 1919. Britain had been involved in a very long war with the Triple Alliance and the armistice had been called one month prior to the pioneering flight, so many in the military were showing, at the very least, signs of trauma, which was named battle fatigue in WW2 and it was not until the 1980s that PTSD was recognised as a disorder. It is unknown what psychological impact the war had on Brown, but what we do know is documented and the purpose of this book is to celebrate what he achieved and keep it as a record of honour to him and his fellow crew members. The journey of Sergeant Brown is without a doubt a story of bravery and immense courage and this narrative will give some insight into Thomas Brown's early life in the Flying Corps and RAF during his time of service.

Happy Reading

# PART ONE

# BEGINNINGS

Sergeant Thomas Brown was born on the 18th of August 1888 in Nine Mile Burn, near Penicuik, Midlothian in Scotland. He had one sister. He Qualified as Carpenter in July 1908 and then trained as a draughtsman. Thomas Brown then served in the Royal Flying Corps/Royal Air Force from 1915-1920.

*Monksburn cottage, Nine Mile Burn, Midlothian. Thomas Brown's childhood home near Penicuik.*

# FIRST EVER FLIGHT UNITED KINGDOM TO INDIA

This highly significant event in Brown's life took place shortly after WW1 ended, during his time in the Royal Air Force. He was on the very first flight from the United Kingdom to India. Brown joined the Air Corps in 1915. The Royal Flying Corps (RFC) was the air arm of the British Army before and during WW1, until it merged with the Royal Naval Air Service on 1 April 1918 to form the Royal Air Force. After starting in 1914 with some 2,073 personnel, the RAF flourished to 114,000 personnel, and 4,000 combat aircraft over 150 squadrons.

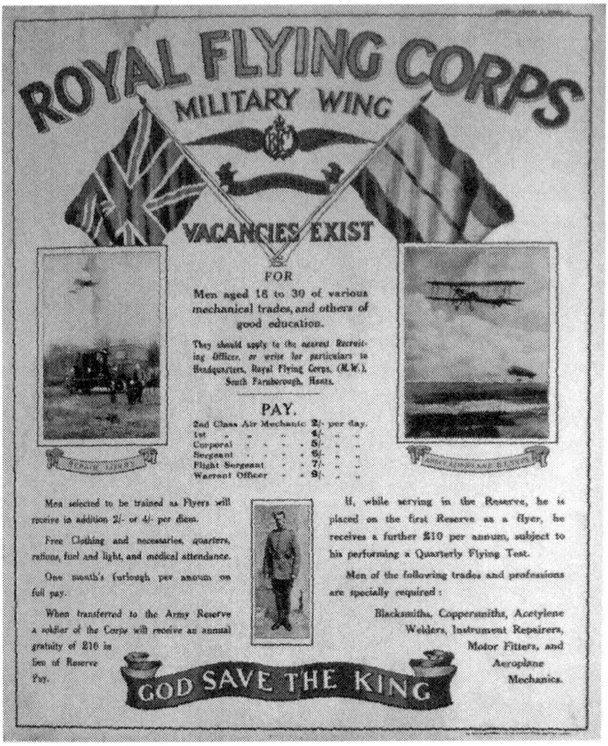


*Recruiting poster*

# THE FLIGHT CREW

On the 13th of December 1918, Sergeant Thomas Brown left the UK onboard the Old Carthusian, a Handley Page V/1500 biplane. Sergeant Brown was a rigger (mechanic) and part of the flight crew. The pilot was Major Archibald Stuart Charles Stuart-MacLaren. There was also Captain Robert 'Jock' Halley, D.F.C., A.F.C. Jock was born in Perth in November 1895, the second son of Bailie Robert Halley, and was educated at Perth Academy. They were accompanied by Air Vice Marshal Sir Norman Duckworth Kerr McEwan C.B. C.M.G., D.S.O., R.A.F. And there were two fitters, Flight Sergeant Smith and Sergeant Crockett. There was also Tiny, a dog, but more about him later. At least four of the crew were Scots born which guaranteed some proverbial banter on the flight.

They set off from Martlesham Heath in Woodbridge, Suffolk, their route to take them to Rome, Malta, Cairo, Baghdad, and Karachi, India on the 15th of January 1919. Then finally they would fly into Delhi the following day.

# EXPERIENCES OF THOMAS BROWN AND THE FLIGHT CREW ABOARD THE HANDLEY PAGE V/1500 HEAVY BOMBER, J1936, HMA OLD CARTHUSIAN

Captain Robert Halley and Major Stuart Maclaren piloted the first flight to India from the United Kingdom on Friday December the 13th 1918. They took off from Martlesham Heath in Suffolk and finally arrived in India on the 15th of January 1919. It was an early pioneer flight and as such the crew met with some amusing, interesting, and frightening circumstances.

The crew aboard the Old Carthusian were a carefully selected team. Captain Halley had been a night bomber with Naval 'A' Squadron formed in haste at Manston in 1917 and equipped with twin-engine Handley Page 0/100 bombers and sent out to Ochey aerodrome – near Nancy in the Vosges district of France – to bomb the Rhine towns. This was after the Germans had bombed London and south-east England and civilians called for retaliation.

The squadron was later 16 Naval and then No. 216 Squadron Royal Air Force and joined the independent air force formed under Major General Hugh Trenchard at the time.

Captain Halley was pulled away from this very mission on orders to report to Colonel Mulock at Air Headquarters in London. He was given very little information about the new assignment, but the speed and secrecy told him it was important. His orders had come from brigade headquarters with a letter from General Newall mentioning 'the right spot', which he took to mean a raid on Berlin. His journey took him by road to the Naval Office in Paris and onto Dunkirk, then by destroyer to Dover where a waiting car took him to London. On delivering the letter to Colonel Mulock, he was told the plan. He was to go immediately to Bircham Newton in Norfolk where Handley Page V/1500s were being readied for a special, and very secret, assignment.

He arrived at Bircham Newton after dark, but the station was a hive of industry with people working on the giant HPs. He reported to Colonel Babington, the CO., who confirmed the raid on Berlin and named his co-pilot as captain Darby and the four other pilots as Major Brackley, Major Darley, Major Digby (who had been in Naval "A" with him) and another pilot.

They were confined to camp with everything devoted to

planning the raid. Hostilities were lasting longer than expected, so big bomber attacks were planned against Berlin and other objectives for which V/1500s were designed and built. They were bigger than anything built by the British before and their wingspan at 126 feet approached that of the Super-fortress of WW2. They had four Rolls-Royce engines at a combined 1400hp, 5ft diameter undercarriage wheels, a fuel capacity of I000 gallons, weighed 13.5 tons, and had a top speed of 100mph.

But during this excitement the armistice was declared, so plans for bombing Berlin had to change. However, they found out that they would never have got to Berlin, as during a test flight without bombs Digby failed to get off the ground and crashed into a field outside the aerodrome.

A couple of days later, Colonel Mulock arrived with Captain Halley who was joined by Major MacLaren and given orders to take a Handley Page to India. They headed to Martlesham Heath where the mechanics were working on the aircraft and from where their journey would start. The remainder of the crew for the flight to end the third Afghan war and to go to India were there. Flight Sergeants Smith and Crockett were the fitters, Sergeant Brown was the rigger, and general MacEwan was a passenger who was to take over as AOC upon arrival in India. The plane was christened HMA *Old Carthusian* owing to MacEwen and MacLaren both schooling at Charterhouse. And the final passenger was Tiny, a Maltese terrier who belonged to MacLaren. Tiny had flown to Egypt earlier in the year and was really keen on flying, running to the ladder as soon as the engine roared to be taken into the cockpit.

Their first attempt at taking the Handley Page to India was on December the 8th 1918. However, after fifteen minutes in the air and flying at 800ft the starboard engine's reduction gear packed in, so they had to return to Martlesham. Although the flight was secret, the morning after they returned a sinister-looking man was outside their bedroom waiting. He proceeded to follow them around, hoping to get some information. It was later discovered he was a *Daily Mail* reporter wanting a scoop.

It took the Rolls-Royce mechanics five days to fit new gears, but the crew took off again on the 13th, heading for Le Bourget Aerodrome, Paris.

*December 13th 9:55 a.m.*

*We passed over Harwich and it was interesting to see all the surrendered German submarines lying in the stream with the light cruiser squadron ahead, guarding their prey.*

*From SGT Thomas Brown's Diary*

. . .

Not long after take-off they were above clouds on the other side of the Channel and flew for three hours without seeing land. When they tried to get through the clouds they were met with a rainstorm with no visibility, so they climbed and steered North. Concerned they may be over the North Sea, they were relieved when a hole in the clouds revealed land below. They flew through the gap and shortly found themselves at Bergues aerodrome, near Dunkirk, feeling greatly relieved. The next day they flew to Paris, landing at Le Bourget.

*December 14th 9.45 am*

*We were somewhat astounded to hear that an account of our proposed journey to India had appeared in the Paris Daily Mail that morning saying that we had left Martlesham the previous day and had been forced by fog to land near the coast. How this information got out, we are at a loss to explain, unless the Daily Mail correspondent who dogged our footsteps at Ipswich, employed the methods of Mr. and Mrs. Zen zig, or a friend on the telephone exchange. In any case, in spite of instructions that our trip was to be kept secret, it was all over Paris before we arrived.*

*From SGT Thomas Brown's Diary*

. . .

On the 15th they set off for St Miramas aerodrome near Marseilles but ran into low cloud and poor visibility. After their previous experience, they decided to land at Beaune, where they remained for two days until the fog had lifted. The host of the hotel where they stayed was also the owner of a vineyard, so kindly brought a fine magnum of Burgundy for them.

On the 18th they set out for Rome but ran into bad weather again and were brought down in Pisa by a heavy rainstorm. Otranto on the Adriatic coast was their aim on the 19th but the plane failed to climb over the Apennines, so they tried to go around the 'toe' of Italy. However, through the straits they ran into some unusual atmospheric conditions and dropped 200ft in a vacuum turning 180° in the process. Encountering a strong headwind and seeing they were short on fuel to get to Otranto, they headed for the aerodrome at Catania in Sicily. Darkness was falling fast but from above the aerodrome looked good, so they went in to land. But on landing they were up to their axles in in a bog and the plane almost went over onto its nose. Luckily the Sicilian Army turned up to dig them out, but it took a whole day and it put them off their intended route.

They decided to try for Malta next. The only landing ground there was The Marsa where there was a small race course. The flight crew heard that they could get English petrol there. Fortunately, there was a strong north-west wind blowing and they just made a dusk landing. Having been warned that this favourable wind would only last another half day, they decided to push on through the night. To get an extra fifty yards the army took down a wall to aid their take off. Also, around the race course ran a low bank which Captain Halley used to place a red lantern on, so they could hoist the plane before striking it. On the other side was a decline, which would help with gathering height. They took off at 2am and made for the North African coast, aiming to land at 6am.

*December 21st.*

*At 6:30 a.m. the sun appeared above the horizon and at 6:50 a.m. we crossed the coastline of Africa, 2 miles south of the spot we had set our course for – a very satisfactory piece of Navigation at the end of 420 miles across the sea, which had taken us 3 hours, 48 minutes._Thermos flasks were produced and the occasion was celebrated with cocoa. The engines were running well, far better on the English Petrol which had been procured at Malta, and everything seemed most hopeful for a successful trip.*

*From SGT Thomas Brown's Diary*

. . .

However, on the way to Cairo a reduction gear packed in, so they altered their course for Alexandria. Then inland, somewhere between Sallum and Matruh, a section reduction gear went. With only two engines, they had no choice but to land in the scrub and pray they made it. Textbook it wasn't, but they landed intact and got out to see three Arabs coming toward them. Somehow, MacLaren had just enough Arabic to make them understand his wish to get a message to the nearest British garrison at Matruh and ask them for help.

Before starting the trip, General MacEwan had the sense of mind to ask the Chancellor of the Exchequer for some gold sovereigns, knowing they would be invaluable were they to land in an Arab country. They were given two hundred. They sent the three Arabs off with a sovereign each with the promise of another when they returned.

At night, the temperature in the western desert plummeted. The six huddled together in the fuselage, cursing the cold. By late afternoon the next day, two Ford vans arrived, one driven by a British Corporal and the other by an Egyptian and with them were the three Arabs. They were taken to Garrison headquarters at Matruh where Colonel Bosanquet gave them a very welcome meal. In the middle of it, and without warning, MacEwan said, "Gad! We must get to Cairo tomorrow, it's Christmas!"

So as soon as the meal was finished, the Colonel put them

back on the Ford vans and they went on to Cairo, suffering minor bumps caused by the vehicles accidentally going off-road in the dark. They arrived at Shepheard's Hotel at 7pm on Christmas day and had a wonderful party.

General, MacLaren and Captain Halley had a lovely few days relaxing in the hotel while Sergeant Brown and the other two mechanics repaired the plane in the desert with the help of a working party from Aboukir. The *Old Carthusian* arrived in Cairo in good order on the 1st of January.

At 3am on the 8th, they took off from Heliopolis aerodrome in Cairo intending to fly directly to Baghdad, but as they neared the river Euphrates water in the petrol collector box forced them to land. On the ground near Abu Kamel they cleaned all the filters and took off again. Due to the dark, another landing had to be made on a camel track near Khan Baghdadi, so they flew to Baghdad the next morning. They spent three days in Baghdad having the leading edges of the rear propellers repaired and balanced

after they were damaged by odd bits of metal shed from the rotor vanes of the fuel pumps.

On the 11th they made the hop from Baghdad to Bushire, but a strengthening rod on the wind vane cover came adrift in the air and they had to land in Ahwaz. Seeing a good level spot of country, they aimed the plane towards it, but as they got closer they saw a large formation of cavalry and horse-drawn wagons so landed parallel with the troops. Unfortunately, their landing had caused chaos with horses stampeding in all directions. On exiting the airraft, an irate general, purple in the face with rage, rode alongside and let them have his opinion of the crew's behaviour in dispersing his ceremonial parade. Leaving General MacEwan to handle the situation, the rest of the crew quietly retired behind the *Old Carthusian.* Although not showing any badges of rank when he introduced himself and explained the reason for their emergency landing, the inspecting officer calmed down and went off less purple in the face.

Repairs were done quickly, and they carried on to Bushire for the night. The leg from Bushire to Bandar Abbas was flown on January 12th, and from Bandar Abbas to Karachi on the following day. However, fifty miles outside Karachi another engine went and they were forced to land at Ormara, but not an aerodrome, rather a spit of sand running from the mainland to a 500ft high rock with a tiny village at its base. Back then Ormara was in India, not Pakistan as it is now, so they had technically already made it to India. Fortunately, the sand was wet and they landed safely but finished up with the starboard wings hanging at an angle over one of the village huts. It was a close shave. No sooner had they come to rest when an Indian with a tarboosh came up and said, "I'm a representative of the Eastern Telegraph Company, can I help you?" Later, this man was to give them the most valuable assistance.

They managed to let headquarters in India, Egypt, and the Air Ministry know they'd had a forced landing, and to keep in communication by landline. In sight of Karachi with only 100-150 miles to go and after coping successfully with so many incidents, they were in a most unfortunate and depressing situation with no hope of reaching their target.

General MacEwen was feeling very ill due to sunstroke, so a cable was sent to Karachi requesting a ship to collect him. The Royal Indian Navy sent a sloop called the *Britomart.* Then, as soon as the General left, something miraculous happened. The wind changed direction 180° and was blowing from the mainland, increasing in velocity. The crew went into a huddle and decided that the slope of the beach would counteract the effect of having two engines on one side and only one on the other. Furthermore, if everything possible was jettisoned and only Flight Sergeant Smith remained in the rear cockpit to balance the aircraft, with God on their side, the aircraft might take off.

With the telegraph man organising the villagers and Halley dashing back to get their kit and pay the bills, MacLaren taxied his way between the dunes as fast as he dared fearing they'd stick in the sand. The tide was right out leaving a two-mile strip of firm beach. There was a slope across its width, but two good engines counteracted any swing. The crew of *Old Carthusian* were effecting the kind of take-off that hadn't been done before and with an underpowered and damaged aircraft.

MacLaren opened up the three engines and the aircraft slowly rolled away, gradually picking up speed until airborne after a run of about a mile. They were clear of the village and headed into the wind, which had increased to nearly 40mph. Twenty minutes later at 1,000 feet they passed the *Britomart* on their starboard side. Her smoke was still a smudge on the horizon, when both starboard engines gave a few splutters and stopped, leaving them to defy gravity by the sole efforts of the front port. The wind-driven pump transferring fuel from the main tank to the starboard gravity tank had failed. Halley dived back to the engineer's station and attacked the emergency pump with both hands. The engines picked up again and Halley ran back to the cockpit. He had just managed to get through to Smith – 60 feet to the rear – by sign language when the engines stopped again, and he rushed back to the pumps. As the engines picked up for the second time, Smith came crawling down the fuselage and they took turns to man the pumps.

In the East, darkness falls rapidly with very little twilight for warning. Forty miles short of Karachi with the light of day almost gone, the rear starboard engine began to lose revolutions, its temperature shot up and there was no alternative but to throttle it right down, then switch off completely. Fortunately, it was one on the side with two remaining, so they were left with one on each side, otherwise it would have meant abandoning the plane.

The next half hour seemed like an eternity to the crew. It was impossible to maintain height. With both remaining engines at full throttle and their temperatures almost at boiling point, MacLaren held the aircraft barely above the stall at 52 mph. She staggered along, losing about ten feet of vital altitude every minute. They just scraped over the ridge of hills to the west of Karachi and looked for somewhere to land. They had to hit the ground soon, with no time to circle around looking for the city's temporary aerodrome.

The priority departure signal despatched by Brown in Ormara had not only arrived but was sent straight away by runner to the Chief Royal Engineer officer who was playing hockey. He appreciated the need for urgent action, so grabbed some men and improvised flares from petrol and rags, laying a line of fire by pouring gallons of petrol onto the ground. They then fired off a few pyrotechnics as soon as the faint drone of engines was heard to the west. The plane was losing height, but now they would know what to head for.

Knowing that there might be some high ground on their approach into Karachi they fired a flare ahead and downwards to illuminate the ground. From the flight deck of *Old Carthusian,* the crew peered at the myriad lights of Karachi still some miles away and wondered where they could safely put down. Then Halley gave a wild shout and pointed straight ahead. He had spotted one of the signals, and faintly twinkling on the ground almost dead in line with their heading, was a flare-path. They were now frighteningly low down and the straight-in approach had to be exactly right first time. MacLaren made a skilfully judged approach and a good landing with both engines full out. When the Handley Page rolled to a halt the pilots climbed out, grabbed one another by the arms and danced for joy.

Looking back Captain Halley said, "Until that moment I thought that dancing for joy was just a figure of speech," he recalled, "but we did it – though since we were such an oddly sized couple the onlookers probably thought we were quite mad. They had seen us make a good and apparently normal landing but knew nothing of our harrowing experience."

Modern day jet passengers bothered by the effect of long distance travel on their body clock may care to reflect that this first England to India flight over a distance of 5,560 miles was accomplished in 72 hours 41 minutes, at an average speed of 77mph, total flying time.

That night Halley underlined the impression that flyers were eccentric people by arriving for dinner with the Governor of Sind half an hour late and wearing a dinner suit nearly a foot too long in the sleeves and leg. He had fallen asleep in his bath from sheer exhaustion and was not the easiest to fit when it came to borrowed clothes.

When MacEwan arrived with Brown and Crockett and heard the full story he promptly forestalled any criticism of the pilots by signalling Air Ministry, saying that he could not speak too highly of their enterprise, grit and determination for successfully completing the flight in the face of so many difficulties, particularly during the final 170 miles, of which for over fifty of them there was no possibility of landing.

Despite only once being able to land at the aerodrome designated on their flight plan, the crew had nearly always managed to notify some authority of their whereabouts before anxiety was roused. The aircraft was posted as missing for a short time after the forced landing in Egypt, since it had not been sighted after passing Sallum, and H.Q. Middle East was about to launch a major search when the message reporting its safety was received.

Although their ultimate destination was Delhi, they had nevertheless accomplished a through-flight from England to India. Sergeant Thomas Brown was the only rigger on this crew alongside two fitters, these three stalwart NCO mechanics performing a wonderful job. When one considers that on landing their work had only just begun, it is impossible to praise them enough. At every stop, they had to fill the aircraft with 1,000 gallons of fuel by means of four-gallon cans through a chamois leather funnel filter. The flight crew had left on Friday the 13th December 1918 and arrived on the 15th January 1919 – and they never once landed at their intended destination! Having then flown on to Delhi, where a crowd of 30,000 including the Viceroy greeted the *Old Carthusian* – then having undertaken some VIP flights – Halley was summoned by General McEwan in light of the mounting troubles on the frontier and was ordered to carry out a daring bombing strike on Kabul.

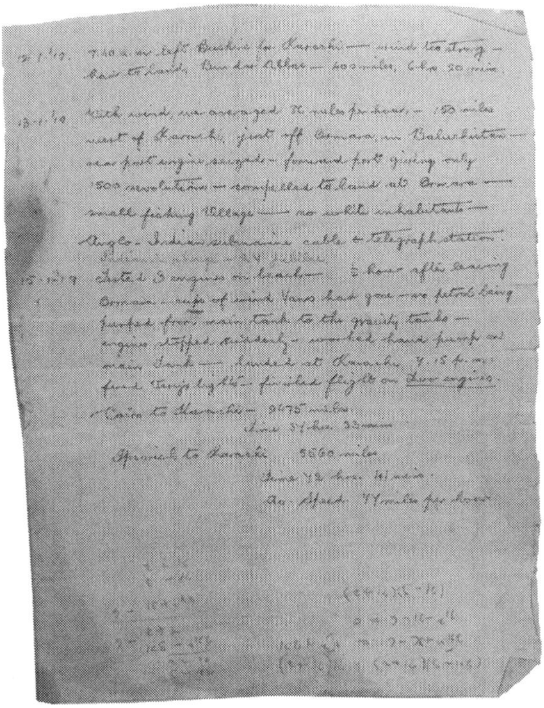

12.1.19. 7.40 a.m. left Bushire for Karachi — wind too strong — had to land Bundar Abbas — 400 miles, 6 hrs 20 mins.

13.1.19. With wind, we averaged 75 miles per hour, — 150 miles west of Karachi, just off Ormara, in Baluchistan — rear port engine seized — forward port giving only 1500 revolutions — compelled to land at Ormara — small fishing village — no white inhabitants — Anglo-Indian submarine cable & telegraph station.

15.1.19. Started 3 engines on beach — ½ hour after leaving Ormara — caps of wind vanes had gone — no petrol being pumped from main tank to the gravity tanks — engine stopped suddenly — worked hand pump on main tank — landed at Karachi 4.15 p.m. — found Verey's lights — finished flight on two engines.

Cairo to Karachi — 2475 miles.
time 37 hrs. 33 mins

Heliopolis to Karachi 5560 miles
time 72 hrs. 41 mins.
Av. Speed 77 miles per hour

*The above letter was written by Sergeant Brown and details Old Carthusian's landing in Karachi with only two working engines.*

# PART 2

# PREPARATIONS IN DELHI AND THE RESURRECTION OF CARTHUSIAN

When *Old Carthusian* landed on a flat stretch of ground on the outskirts of Karachi on January the 15th 1919 and then Delhi with two engines out of four serviceable, the crew had completed the first through flight from England to India. Owing to the state of the engines and the need for extensive repairs to the airframe, it was necessary to station the plane in Karachi for this work to be completed. MacLaren had to return to England due to illness, which left Captain Halley in charge.

*Handley Page V/1500 J1936 HMA Old Carthusian at Karachi*

Four new Rolls-Royce Eagle VIII engines and a range of spares had arrived from Egypt. The engines were installed, and the airframe given an overhaul. As all this work had to be done in the open with makeshift equipment, the crew achieved miracles in getting the aircraft serviceable. While this was going on the Army provided a round-the-clock guard. On tests after the work was completed, they gave the Governor of Sind and several senior officials flights over and around Karachi. They very much appreciated it and in return the crew received some excellent hospitality.

They set out across the Sind Desert to Nasirabad. It was a hot and bumpy passage, and the sun scorched their faces. One night was spent at Nasirabad, where the Maharajah and a few Indian Princes visited the *Old Carthusian* and were very impressed. Sir Charles Kesteven, one of the Viceroy's senior political advisers, had come from Delhi to make the last flight with the crew to the capital.

During the time *Old Carthusian* was being overhauled in Karachi, they spent a few days in Delhi. They were given a wonderful time and many invitations had to be turned down. Arriving into the city early, they flew around giving encouragement to thousands on foot, bicycles and cars making their way along the dusty road to the flat ridge outside the city. On landing they were greeted by the Commander in Chief of India (Sir Charles Monroe) the High Commissioner, and a host of VIPs.

They were kept busy, as the Viceroy had arranged with General MacEwen for the Legislative Council and senior officials to be given flights over and around Delhi. One morning, the Maharajah of Udaipur arrived with his considerable retinue. The cockpits could take eight to ten people, but a few extra had climbed into the rear cockpits, so on taking off they found great difficulty in getting the tail off the ground. It was fortunate that it was the under-carriage that carried away a telegraph line and not the propellers. Looking back at the box tail, they also saw that it was tangled with yards of coloured turban cloth, and it was lucky they landed safely with the material tangled around the elevators.

They also flew Sir Edward Buck, Reuter's agent with the

Indian Government, from Delhi to Ambala. The only available landing area was a golf course, but due to the falling darkness they could not see the bunkers and other hazards. They did land but weren't very popular with the greenkeepers.

Finally, they flew from Ambala to Lahore on the 17th of March, landing at the Aircraft Park where hundreds of spectators had gathered to greet them. *Old Carthusian* had now completed its job and would be left out in the open before being dismantled. A part was put in Delhi Museum and the fuselage, a maze of cross-bracing and struts, was for many years used in the annual sports obstacle race, when competitors had to enter one end and, after some difficulty, emerge from the other.

About this time the frontier tribes were in revolt and uniting under King Amanullah of Afghanistan were attacking India all along the North West Frontier. Troops from Mesopotamia being repatriated home were being diverted to the frontier and the Army in India was being stretched to the limit, hardly able to contain the rising. Places like Peshawar and other key points inside the Indian frontier were under attack.

The Commander in Chief decided to bomb Kabul by air, but there were no aircraft in India capable of the long flight. Two pilots called Biffy Borton and Ross Smith suggested to General MacEwen that a Handley Page 0/400 that was in pieces in Lahore could be reassembled and flown by them for the raid. But they were busy surveying the Calcutta-Port Darwin route to Australia on board the Indian Navy's gunboat *Sphinx* and had run into difficulties, putting ashore on an island with no communication.

Permission was granted by Air Ministry to use the 0/400 and, even though it was positive they could use the plane, it would be a dangerous mission over tough mountain territory in Afghanistan.

The aircraft was tested with a flight to Risalpur and ran faultlessly. They knew Kabul was a very important target and if they were successful it would help the Indian government greatly. In Risalpur there was a dust storm and the 0/400 had to be lashed down. During a lull, they went to see how the plane was faring. It was upturned with the starboard side crushed in and its back broken. It looked as if it had been flipped and then pushed along by a bulldozer. There wouldn't be any bombing of Kabul in that aircraft. The thought crossed their minds, Could the *Old Carthusian*, now condemned, take on this job?

The *Old Carthusian* was not intended to fly again. It had endured heavy treatment on the flight out from England, the centre section undergoing abnormal stress due to forced landings. In Lahore, it had been parked in the open for five months in temperatures of 100+°F, which were terrible conditions for an aircraft built of wood and fabric.

But, General MacEwen was to be onboard the *Old Carthusian* doing the raid on Kabul and said that anything required would be given top priority.

*Two views of the wrecked H.P. 0/400 C9700 at Risalpur in April 1919.*

On returning to Lahore they asked the NCOs including Brown what chance there was of *Old Carthusian* being made serviceable for the Kabul raid. The expression on their faces said everything. However, after they heard the serious conditions along the frontier and how the Commander in Chief was relying on the raid, they decided to make every effort to get the aircraft serviceable. Another obstacle was that a height of 8,000ft needed to be reached to cross a ridge of mountains on the way to Kabul – a height never attained by the *Old Carthusian*.

All work on the aircraft had to be done in the open in daytime temperatures of 100°F (38c). The wings, fuselage and fabric were too hot to work on until the sun had gone down. There were many repairs needed including tightening of fabric, fuselage members braced, wing ribs replaced, wings and fuselage doped, and an aircraft tune-up. Four 112Ib bomb racks were installed on the lower wing spars and operated in conjunction with a bomb sight fitted in the front cockpit. Sixteen 20Ib bombs were stacked in the mid-cockpit, to be dropped through the bottom doorway by the crew, when they to their surprise saw a 112lb bomb that had been left inside a rack on the wing. Also, all lighting in the cockpit was taken out.

A week of work and the plane was ready for testing, so a signal was sent to headquarters Simla. General McEwan and Major Dolphin took it for the test run, but were unable to get the aircraft above 2,700ft. Some more adjustments were needed and a further test.

Two days later they reached 6,700ft. They reported this to

HQ, saying that they would attempt the raid early the following morning. They asked for the help of a bomb aimer who would assist with the navigation, though they would actually do the job mainly by pilot-navigation. A young Lieutenant called Ted Villiers volunteered for the job. He was later to become famous and to receive a knighthood.

# PART 3

# ENDING THE THIRD AFGHAN WAR

"History is defined by achievement, such as the legacy of Thomas Brown."

The Anglo-Afghan Wars had three conflicts (1839-42; 1878-80; and 1919) in which Great Britain, from its base in India, sought to extend its control over neighbouring Afghanistan and oppose Russian influence there. The Anglo-Afghan Wars happened because Britain was concerned that Tsarist forces would attack India via Afghanistan, so they tried to impose their will on Kabul.

The end of the Second Afghan War in 1880 marked the beginning of forty years of good relations between Britain and Afghanistan under the leadership of Abdur Rahman Khan and Habibullah Khan, during which time the British attempted to manage Afghan foreign policy through the payment of a large subsidy. Ostensibly, the country remained independent, but under the Treaty of Gandamak (1879) it accepted that in external matters it would "...have no windows looking on the outside world, except towards India."

In 1901 Emir Abdur Rahman Khan died and his successor, Habibullah, was a pragmatic leader who sided with Britain or Russia, depending on Afghan interests. He was able to maintain a policy of non-involvement throughout the WW1, resisting considerable pressure from the Ottoman Empire when it entered the conflict on the side of Imperial Germany and the Sultan (as titular leader of Islam) called for a holy war against the Allies.

Despite remaining neutral in the conflict, Habibullah accepted a Turkish-German mission in Kabul and military assistance from the central powers as he attempted to play both sides of the conflict for the best deal. By the time the Turco-German mission left Kabul in 1916, it had successfully convinced Habibullah that Afghanistan was an independent nation and should not be beholden to anyone. He failed to keep in check tribal leaders undermining British rule in India, as Turkish agents attempted to provoke trouble along the frontier.

With the end of WW1, Habibullah sought to gain reward from the British government for his assistance during the war. Looking for British recognition of Afghanistan's independence in foreign affairs, he demanded a seat at the Versailles Peace Conference in 1919. This request was denied by the Viceroy on the grounds that attendance at the conference was confined to the belligerents. Further negotiations were scheduled, but before they began Habibullah was assassinated on 19th February 1919.

Habibullah's brother Nasrullah Khan proclaimed himself as Habibullah's successor, while in Kabul, Amanullah, Habibullah's third son also proclaimed himself Amir. The Afghan army suspected Amanullah's complicity in the death of his father. Upon seizing the throne in April 1919 and needing a way of cementing his power, Amanullah posed as a man of democratic ideals, promising reforms in the system of government. He stated that there should be no forced labour, tyranny or oppression and that Afghanistan should be free and independent and no longer bound by the Treaty of Gandamak. He had his uncle Nasrullah arrested for Habibullah's murder and sentenced to life imprisonment. Nasrullah had been the leader of a more conservative element in Afghanistan and his treatment rendered Amanullah's position as Amir somewhat tenuous. By April 1919 he realised that if he could not find a way to placate the conservatives, he would be unlikely to maintain his hold on power. Looking for a diversion from the internal strife in the Afghan court and sensing an advantage in the rising civil unrest in India following the

Amritsar massacre, Amanullah decided to invade British India. In his coronation address, Amānullāh declared total independence from Great Britain. This declaration launched the inconclusive Third Anglo-Afghan War in May 1919.

# OPPOSING FORCES

Fighting was confined to a series of skirmishes between an ineffective Afghan army and a British Indian army exhausted from the heavy demands of WWI. In 1919 the Afghan regular army was not a formidable force and was only able to muster 50,000 men. These men were organised into 21 cavalry regiments and 75 infantry battalions with about 280 modern artillery pieces, organised into 70 batteries. In addition, however, the Afghan command could call upon the loyalty of up to 80,000 frontier tribesmen and an indeterminate number of deserters from local militia units under British command. In reality, the Afghan regular army was not ready for war. As in past years, the upper levels of the officer corps were riddled with political intrigue. In his book on the campaign, Lieutenant-General George Molesworth gave the following evaluation of the Amir's army:

Afghan regular units were ill-trained, ill-paid, and probably under strength. The cavalry was little better than indifferent infantry mounted on equally indifferent ponies. Rifles varied between modern German, Turkish and British types, to obsolete Martinis and Snyders. Few infantry units had bayonets. Artillery was pony-drawn, or pack, and included modern 10cm Krupp howitzers, 75mm Krupp mountain guns and ancient seven pounder weapons. There were a few, very old, four-barrel Gardiner machine guns. Ammunition was in short supply and distribution must have been very difficult. For the artillery much black powder was used, both as a propellant and bursting charge for shells. The Kabul arsenal workshops were elementary and mainly staffed by Sikh artificers with much ingenuity but little real skill. There was no organised transport, and arrangements for supply were rudimentary.

In support of the regulars, the Afghan command expected to call out the tribes, which could gather 20-30,000 Afridi fighters in the Khyber region alone. In stark contrast to the regulars, the tribal Lashkars were probably the best troops that the Afghans had – excellent fighters, well-armed with weapons made themselves or stolen from the garrisons, and with plenty of ammunition. In meeting this threat, the British could call on a much larger force. In May 1919 the British and British Indian Army, not including frontier militia, totalled eight divisions, as well as five independent brigades of infantry and three of cavalry. However, of this force, the entire North-West Frontier Province had only three infantry divisions and two cavalry brigades (although there was also GHQ India's central reserve of one infantry division and one cavalry brigade). From this they formed a striking force of two infantry divisions and two cavalry brigades for offensive operations on the Kyber front with the possibility of using it also in the Tochi and Kurram areas. One infantry division and a so-called "mounted" brigade were also detailed for operations on the Baluchistan-Zhob front. There were also three frontier brigades as well as some frontier militia and irregular corps and artillery were also in short supply.

But the main problem for the British was discontent among their soldiers. The troops in India were no longer as uncritical as they had been when considering what they were being asked to do. Like other units of the British Army, many of the troops considered the war over and looked forward to being demobilised. The Indian Army had been heavily committed to WW1 and had suffered a large number of casualties. Many of its units still had not returned from overseas, and those that had returned had begun the process of demobilisation and as such many regiments had lost almost all their most experienced men. Likewise, the British Army in India had been gutted. Before 1914, there had been 61 British regiments serving in India. However, ten (two cavalries and eight infantry) had been withdrawn to fight in Europe or the Middle East. In their place, units of the Territorial Army – part-time soldiers usually only intended for home defence but who had volunteered for overseas service – had been sent in order to release regular units for the fighting in France. After four years of mundane garrison duty away from their families and disaffected, most of these men were really only interested in demobilisation and returning to Britain to get on with their lives. They were in no way prepared for a hard-fought campaign on the Indian frontiers.

# CAUSE OF THE WAR

The conflict began on the 3rd of May 1919 when Afghan troops crossed the frontier at the western end of the Khyber Pass and captured the town of Bagh. Bagh was strategically crucial to the British and Indians as it provided water to Landi Kotal, which was garrisoned by just two companies of British Indian Army troops. Although initially considered a minor border infraction, this attack was actually part of the broader invasion plan. The attack had been launched ahead of schedule, as Amanullah had intended initially to time it to coincide with an uprising that was being planned in Peshawar for the 8th May. This forewarned the British Chief Commissioner of the North West Frontier, Sir George Roos-Keppel, and he was able to successfully convince the Viceroy, Lord

Chelmsford, of the need to respond to the occupation of Bagh before it led to further unrest in Peshawar.

In response, the British Indian government declared war upon Afghanistan on the 6th of May and ordered a general mobilisation of the British and Indian forces. It was decided that the two companies of Sikhs and Gurkhas that had been sent to Landi Kotal needed to be reinforced, however, the mobilization process had only just begun and at that stage there was only one battalion available for this. So, on the 7th of May the second Battalion, Somerset Light Infantry, were brought up clandestinely through the Khyber Pass aboard a convoy of 37 lorries.

Meanwhile, demands were made for the population to hand over the uprising's ringleaders with threats that the city's water supply would be cut. The inhabitants complied, and by dawn on the 8th May the situation in the city was under control and the threat of an uprising abated.

By this stage, more reinforcements were available and the garrison at Landi Kotal grew to brigade-size with the arrival of the rest of the 1st Infantry Brigade under Brigadier GD Crocker. On the 9th of May the British and Indian troops launched an attack on the Afghans that had seized Bagh the previous week. But the attack failed because the brigade commander decided to split his forces and detach half his force to protect his flank and, as a result, was unable to achieve the necessary concentration of force to capture all of his objectives. The month-long war continued to cost both the Afghan and British army loss of lives until the introduction of British airpower.

## IMPACT MADE BY THE CREW IN ENDING THIRD AFGHAN WAR

Although limited in number and quality, airpower proved to be one of the greatest assets the British possessed during this conflict. Not only did it allow them to extend their reach beyond the border and bomb Kabul, but it also enabled them to harass the retreating enemy and to break up tribesmen as they attempted to form larger groups before launching an attack. The ability of the British to project airpower – even small-scale raids – had considerable psychological effects.

On the 24th of May 1919 a flight crew led by Captain Halley aboard the *Old Carthusian* flew through the Khyber Pass in pre-dawn darkness with observer Lieutenant Ted Villiers. Also aboard were Flight Sergeant Smith and Sergeant Crockett, fitters, and Sergeant Thomas Brown, rigger.

The *Old Carthusian* was armed with a bomb load of four 112-pound (50.8 kg) and sixteen 20-pound (9.1 kg) bombs. The target was the royal palace of Amanullah Khan in Kabul. They took off at 3am on the 24th of May 1919 – Empire Day. An L-shaped flare path was laid out consisting of seven flares made from empty five-gallon oil drums filled with oil-soaked cotton, which proved effective for take-off. The route lay towards the Khyber Pass and as the clearing height was about 3,000 feet this meant flying around for an hour to gain height before going over a ridge of hills. The Khyber was only dimly visible, as were a few lights at Jamrud Fort and Landi Kotal. From there they flew over the Kabul river and a rough road running parallel up to Jalabad, which was the only town of any size on the route. As they were approaching Jalabad and daybreak was coming, Captain Halley checked the starboard rev-counter and saw water leaking from the base of the second cylinder. Flight Sergeant Smith – with engines throttled back to aid hearing – hurriedly conferred as to what should be done.

The leak was caused by a defective rubber connection between the water jacket and the collecting pipe, running along the base of the six cylinders. Drops of water were being blown by the slipstream, making it impossible to estimate the extent of the leakage. Kabul was still about 90 miles ahead, and there was the return time to think about. The *Old Carthusian* was in the middle of a steep turn and looking down the crew noticed smoke from a fire being blown in the direction of Kabul and stretching out parallel with the ground, indicating a favourable wind of some force. Villiers talked with Flight Sergeant Smith and after some shrugging of shoulders, they decided to continue.

Oh God! they gasped, as somewhere ahead there was the ridge to cross, with Kabul further on. They were continually looking at the leak and up at the frightening height of the mountains. The Jagdalak Pass, their route that rose to nearly 8,000 feet, was not yet visible. It was quite thrilling threading their way between high peaks. Suddenly, on making a turn, the road appeared on a crest of the ridge ahead, but to their horror it was some height above the aircraft's nose.

Remembering the smoke they had just left behind, they wondered if they could gain enough up-lift over the hills ahead. At two miles away they were definitely below the ridge and they inwardly said, "here goes" and, holding the nose up with the four engines running full-throttle they sailed over the top and down the other side. The look Villiers had on his face was unbelievable. He quickly looked downwards from his side of the cockpit and with a grin gave a thumbs up. Afterwards, Villiers said that when passing over the ridge he saw a camel convoy of over 100 animals on its way to Kabul stampede in all directions, quite a number falling down the precipitous mountain side.

Once over the ridge and having regained their breath, they saw their target ahead spread out over a vast area on a lush green fertile plateau – a marked change from the barren and mountainous terrain that they had just passed over. With a population of 300,000, it was not surprising that Kabul covered such an area. It was also reputed to have the busiest and finest Bazaar in the East.

Owing to the risk of starboard engine failure, they had to cut their time over Kabul to a minimum. Nevertheless, the bombing achieved positive results. If the sight and sound of the *Old Carthusian* roaring over the city at a few hundred feet with four engines fitted with stub exhausts didn't frighten a city that had never seen an aircraft before, nothing would.

On the return journey they again headed for the Jagdalak Pass and had the benefit of a slightly following wind. As they were now relieved of their bombs, they flew over the ridge with height to spare.

The return flight seemed interminable and they were all very conscious of the water leakage on the starboard engine. Halley's eyes were glued to the temperature gauge in the nacelle and they had nearly reached the Khyber when he saw the pointer rise above normal. There was nothing to do but switch off the engine and carry on with three running full-out to keep height. It worked, and they landed at Risalpur after six hours in the air.

The object of bombing Kabul was to alarm King Amanullah, which was so successful that a message came to the Viceroy immediately afterwards to the effect that the Afghans wanted peace. This was the end of the *Old Carthusian's* career, which had been beset by misfortune from the outset. Nevertheless, the old V/1500 had accomplished something unique in history – it had helped end a war. After the raid, *Old Carthusian* was damaged by termites and never flew again. The fuselage survived as a squadron office at Risalpur.

So, the Third Afghan War was terminated by a strategic bombing raid at a negligible cost, which must have saved hundreds of lives and the cost of an extensive land campaign. It also restored peace to a large slice of India. This single bombing raid is credited with in part ending the war. History will never forget Brown and the crew for this impact.

# PART 4

# PHOTO GALLERY

# COMMENDATIONS FOR THOMAS BROWN

This letter highlights Brown taking part in the flight to India and the flight to Kabul in Afghanistan.

NDK MacEwan Brigadier General of the Commanding Royal Air Force, India, said of Sergeant Thomas Brown, "Flight Sergeant Thomas Brown accompanied me in this flight of the giant Handley Page aeroplane from England to India in December 1918, as an observer. He was most thorough and conscientious in all his work, and he always knew that the machine was as safe as it could be before we left the ground, owing to his careful attention. He always greeted discomfort and disappointment with a cheery heart and made the best of them. I never want to have a more reliable NCC with me on such a trip. This Non-commissioned officer was largely responsible for the successful bombing of Kabul in May 1919, during which he accompanied Captain Halley. I wish him the best of good fortune in the future and thoroughly recommend him for any position of trust and reliability." Sergeant NDK McEwan, Brigadier General, Commanding Royal Air Force, Indi

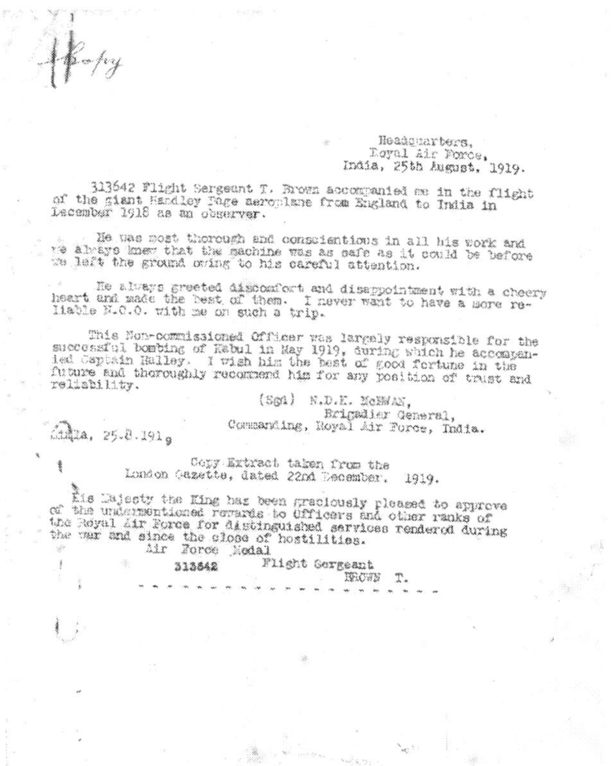

Copy

Headquarters,
Royal Air Force,
India, 25th August, 1919.

313642 Flight Sergeant T. Brown accompanied me in the flight of the giant Handley Page aeroplane from England to India in December 1918 as an observer.

He was most thorough and conscientious in all his work and we always knew that the machine was as safe as it could be before we left the ground owing to his careful attention.

He always greeted discomfort and disappointment with a cheery heart and made the best of them. I never want to have a more reliable N.C.O. with me on such a trip.

This Non-commissioned Officer was largely responsible for the successful bombing of Kabul in May 1919, during which he accompanied Captain Halley. I wish him the best of good fortune in the future and thoroughly recommend him for any position of trust and reliability.

(Sgd) N.D.K. McEWAN,
Brigadier General,
Commanding, Royal Air Force, India.

India, 25.8.1919

Copy Extract taken from the
London Gazette, dated 22nd December. 1919.

His Majesty the King has been graciously pleased to approve of the undermentioned rewards to Officers and other ranks of the Royal Air Force for distinguished services rendered during the war and since the close of hostilities.

Air Force Medal

313642 Flight Sergeant
BROWN T.

- - - - - - - - - - - - - - - - - - - - -

*Copy of extract used by London Gazette*

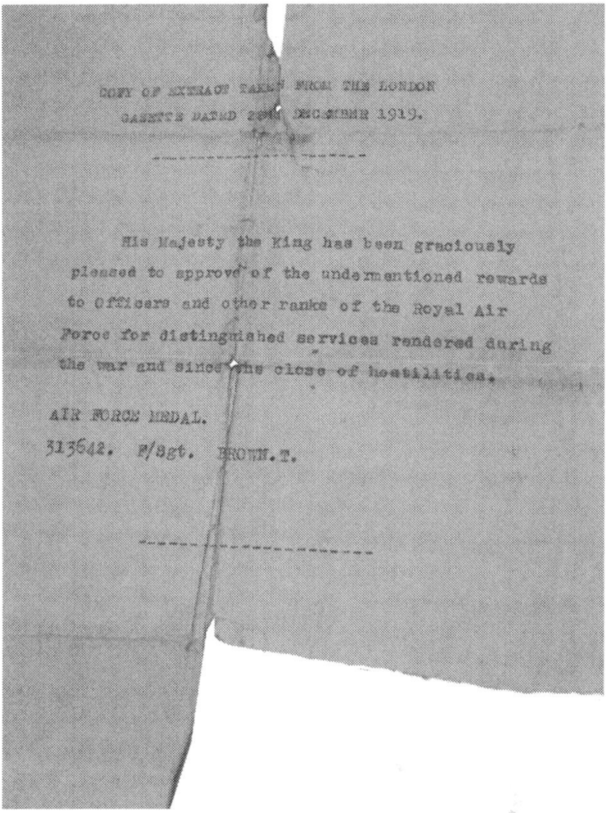

COPY OF EXTRACT TAKEN FROM THE LONDON
GAZETTE DATED [illegible] DECEMBER 1919.

---

His Majesty the King has been graciously pleased to approve of the undermentioned rewards to Officers and other ranks of the Royal Air Force for distinguished services rendered during the war and since the close of hostilities.

AIR FORCE MEDAL.

313642. F/Sgt. BROWN.T.

---

*London Gazette*

# RAF MEDAL

Thomas Brown gained the Air Force medal

*On the rim of the medal it says 313642 SERG BROWN T RAF*

# INVITATION TO SEE THE KING

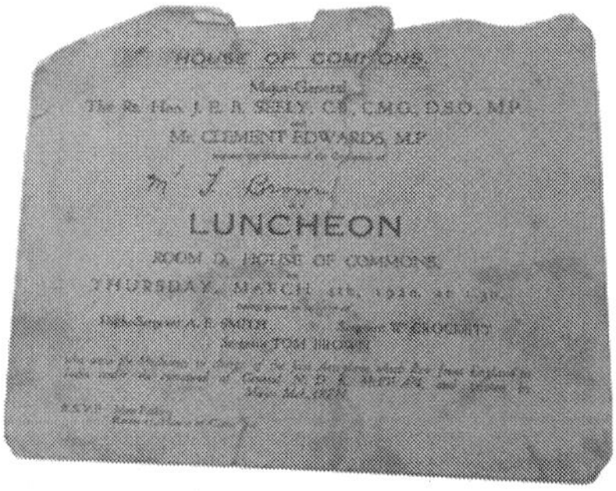
HOUSE OF COMMONS

Major-General

The Rt. Hon. J. E. B. SEELY, C.B., C.M.G., D.S.O., M.P.

Mr. CLEMENT EDWARDS, M.P.

LUNCHEON

ROOM D, HOUSE OF COMMONS

THURSDAY, MARCH

*Photo of actual lunch invitation*

# COMPASS HELMET AND GOGGLES

*The compass used by Brown on the flight to India still works. Photo by Paul Reid 2019.*

*Actual goggles and helmet worn by Sergeant Brown*
*Photo taken 2019*

# CAPTAIN HALLEY'S INTERVIEW QUOTE

Robert 'Jock' Halley quote from an interview in 1979.

"There is one final comment that I would like to make concerning the raid. As the pilot and captain of the aircraft I was given a Second Bar to my Distinguished Flying Cross. However, my stalwart N.C.Os, Flight Sergeant Smith and Sergeant Crockett, fitters, and Sergeant Brown, rigger, who accompanied me quite voluntarily and who had supervised the rebuilding of the aircraft, received no official recognition in spite of all my recommendations. They had all won the Air Force Medal for their efforts on the flight to India. Now, we know that the D.F.C. and D.F.M. are awarded for 'distinguished flying in the face of the enemy,' and the A.F.C. and A.F.M. for 'distinguished flying in the face of Providence!' Surely these brave men had earned some recognition in the former category and Lieutenant Villiers also.

Here, belatedly, let me pay my respects to them"

(*Aeroplane* August 1979, ref).

## THE PLANE

The Handley Page V/1500 first flew on the 22nd of May 1918. The designation comes from the original name, Type 5, combined with the total horsepower of its engines. It was a three-bay biplane with four engines mounted in two nacelles between the upper and lower wings. The bomber was 64 feet, 0 inches (19.507 meters) long with a wingspan of 126 feet, 0 inches (38.405 meters) and was 23 feet, 0 inches (7.010 meters) high. Empty weight was 17,600 pounds (7,983 kilograms), and maximum take-off weight was 30,000 pounds (13,608 kilograms).

They had a wing span of 126ft and four Rolls-Royce engines, between them developing 1,400 h.p., with a fuel capacity of I,000 gal, and had a top speed of 95-100 m.p.h. They weighed 1312 tons and each of the four undercarriage wheels was 5ft in diameter.

Handley page captured in mid-air

# THE ENGINE

*Rolls-Royce Eagle VIII aircraft engine (serial number 5272) at the Smithsonian Institution National Air and Space Museum. (NASM)*

The V/1500 had a maximum speed of 99 miles per hour (159.3 kilometres per hour) at Sea Level, and its service ceiling was 11,000 feet (3,353 meters). It carried fuel to remain airborne for 17 hours. Maximum range was 1,300 miles (2,092 kilometres).

The V/1500 was armed with three .303-caliber Lewis machine guns. The maximum bomb load was 7,500 pounds (3,402 kilograms).

Handley Page built 63 V/1500 bombers. J1936, they were constructed primarily of wood and fabric and eventually succumbed to termites.

# AFTER THE RAF AND MOVE TO DUNDEE

After the RAF, Sergeant Thomas Brown was seconded to Poland with Handley Page at the end of 1919. He then went on to train as a teacher at Moray House, Edinburgh and qualified in 1922. After teaching in Angus, he joined the staff of Rosebank School, Dundee in 1924. He became an assistant headmaster at Brown Street, South Road, Cowgate, Butterburn, Rosebank (where he met his wife Florence who was teaching there) and Hawkhill Primary Schools, and was appointed Headteacher at Downfield School in 1947, and later at Wallacetown School, from which he retired in 1953. He was ordained an elder of St Andrews Church in Dundee and subsequently at St David's North Church, Dundee in 1940. He was a member of the Fabian Society and was involved with the

Dundee branch of India Relief charity. He enjoyed reading and studied the German language. During WW2, he was a fire watch volunteer in Dundee. Having grown up in the countryside, he enjoyed studying wildlife particularly birds and animals.

At forty-three years old he married Florence McRae in 1932. Florence Brown studied at St Andrews university.

Sergeant Thomas Brown died 1973 in Dundee.

## HIS LEGACY - LIVING DESCENDENTS

Thomas and Florence Brown had four daughters, Helen, Florence, Jean, and Johanna. There are ten grandchildren, twenty-one great grandchildren, and thirteen great-great-grandchildren. That's a total of 48 descendants (January 2019).

*Sergeant Thomas Brown's four daughters from left to right:, Johanna, Helen, Jean and Florence. Photo by Paul Reid 2019*

# IN HONOUR OF THE FLIGHT CREW

IN HONOUR OF THE FLIGHT CREW

In Honour of the flight crew:

Major Archibald Stuart Charles Stuart-MacLaren

Captain Robert ("Jock") Halley, D.F.C., A.F.C.,

Air Vice Marshal Sir Norman Duckworth Kerr MacEwen C.B. C.M.G., D.S.O., R.A.F.)

Flight Sergeant Smith

Sergeant Crockett

Sergeant Thomas Brown

# THANKS

To all four of Thomas Brown's daughters for the photos, diaries memorabilia and memories. Bryan Swopes, his website, a treasure chest of aviation history www.thisdayinaviation.com. Paul Reid Photographer, Andrew Palmer for help editing and to Mrs Fiona Stewart for support and encouragement.

## COLLATOR

Collated by Gordon Stewart, Grandson of Thomas Brown. In December 2016, he overheard his nephew Callum Stewart talking about his great grandfather's aviation exploits with Florence Stewart (Gordon's mother), daughter of Thomas Brown and how she had preserved his diaries. After two years he eventually read them and realised how significant this event was and that his achievements no longer could be kept quiet and had to be written about and celebrated.

www.gordonstewart.global

# HELPFUL LINKS

The following websites along with the documents held by family members provided some of the factual information to make this eBook possible.

https://www.rafmuseum.org.uk/research/history-of-aviation-timeline/interactive-aviation-timeline/british-civil-aviation/1919.aspx

Some of the information came from this source. https://www.thisdayinaviation.com/13-december-1918/

https://wikivisually.com/wiki/Handley_Page_V%2F1500

https://defenceoftherealm.wordpress.com/2016/05/24/may-25th-1919-bombing-the-kings-palace-in-kabul/

https://en.wikipedia.org/wiki/Handley_Page_V/1500

http://discovery.nationalarchives.gov.uk/results/r?_q=313642%20thomas%20brown&_ps=30

https://en.wikipedia.org/wiki/India_General_Service_Medal_(1909)

https://www.rafmuseum.org.uk/research/history-of-aviation-timeline/interactive-aviation-timeline/british-civil-aviation/1919.aspx

Quote from Halley, Robert, Group Captain. "Per Ardua ad India." Aeroplane Monthly. V6 N12, December 1978, pp 656-661.

https://en.m.wikipedia.org/wiki/No._216_Squadron_RAF

# VIDEO FOOTAGE

Video footage of Ormara Beach, where the plane landed just before Karachi (modern day Pakistan) https://www.youtube.com/watch?v=qWYGsKcIvtY

Video footage of the Handley Page https://www.youtube.com/watch?v=12OWx9yfCEQ

# QUOTES

Theodore Roosevelt, 1910

It is not the critic who counts; not the man who points out how the strong man stumbles, or where the doer of deeds could have done them better. The credit belongs to the man who is actually in the arena, whose face is marred by dust and sweat and blood; who strives valiantly; who errs, who comes short again and again, because there is no effort without error and shortcoming; but who does actually strive to do the deeds; who knows great enthusiasms, the great devotions; who spends himself in a worthy cause; who at the best knows in the end the triumph of high achievement, and who at the worst, if he fails, at least fails while daring greatly…

Timothy Snyder's book; "On Tyranny: Twenty Lessons from the Twentieth Century," the first sentence in the book is worth noting; "History does not repeat, but it does instruct."

Printed in Great Britain
by Amazon

33492337R00056